Aphids

This book has been reviewed
for accuracy by
Walter L. Gojmerac
Professor of Entomology
University of Wisconsin—Madison.

Library of Congress Cataloging in Publication Data

Heymann, Georgianne.
  Aphids.

  (Nature close-ups)
  Adaptation of: Arimaki / Jun Nanao, Hidetomo Oda.
  Summary: Describes, in text and photographs, the
physical characteristics, life cycle, and habitat
of aphids.
  1. Aphididae—Juvenile literature.   [1. Aphids]
I. Nanao, Jun. Arimaki. II. Title.
QL527.A64H49 1986   595.7'52   86-28017

ISBN 0-8172-2717-2 (lib. bdg.)
ISBN 0-8172-2735-0 (softcover)

This edition first published in 1987 by Raintree Publishers Inc.

Text copyright © 1987 by Raintree Publishers Inc., translated by
Jun Amano from *Aphides* copyright © 1975 by Jun Nanao and
Hidetomo Oda.

Photographs copyright © 1975 by Nanao-Kikaku.

World English translation rights for *Color Photo Books on Nature*
arranged with Kaisei-Sha through Japan Foreign-Rights Center.

1 2 3 4 5 6 7 8 9 0   90 89 88 87 86

Aphids

Adapted by
Georgianne Heymann

Raintree Publishers

Milwaukee

◀ **Aphids on a rose bush.**

The green aphids are hidden against the stem of the rose plant. Different kinds of aphids are different colors. They can be black, reddish brown, orange, or white.

▶ **An aphid colony.**

Aphid colonies are usually found near the tops of young plants where there is a large supply of sap for them to eat.

During a lightly falling spring rain, many small insects cling to a young rose plant. The insects on the plant are so close together that they almost cover the stalks and stems of the rose. It is only when they move that the tiny insects, called aphids, can be clearly seen.

Aphids have soft, pear-shaped bodies about one-eighth of an inch long. They are part of a large group of insects that live by sucking sap from the leaves, stems, and fruits of various plants. Often aphids can be found gathered around the tops of young plants where the supply of sap is the largest. They crowd together in numbers of fifty to a hundred or more.

A plant that a colony of aphids has fed on will eventually lose its healthy green appearance. The leaves of the plant wilt and become covered with brown spots. Soon the plant is left with curled up, wilted leaves and damaged fruits.

Although there are about two thousand different kinds of aphids, a colony is usually made up of only one kind, or species, of aphid. Aphids in all stages of growth are found in the colony. There are small and large, old and young aphids. Some of the aphids have wings and some are wingless. And sure to be among the aphids are other insects that are attracted to the sugary liquid, called honeydew, that most aphids produce.

When an aphid feeds on a plant, it pokes its tube-like mouthparts in-to the plant and sucks out sap. The sap, which is made up of sugars and water, passes through the aphid's gut, or stomach. Most of the sap helps the aphid live and grow. The sap that is not used this way mixes with other waste materials and travels to the end of the aphid's gut. There the mixture, or honeydew, is excreted from the back section of the body, the abdomen, through an opening. Ants, flies, butterflies and bees all like the sweet honeydew excreted by aphids.

8

Usually, insects of one kind begin life in the same way. Aphids, however, are different. Some aphids start their life cycle after coming out of eggs. Other aphid young are born alive.

The first aphids in spring come out of, or emerge from, eggs. They are all wingless females. The next few generations, or groups of young, are wingless females, too. But they do not emerge from eggs, they are born live. Throughout the rest of summer, the female aphids give birth to live young without mating with male aphids.

Many offspring are produced through the summer. There may be as many as thirteen generations in a single summer. As more aphid young are born, they include winged female aphids. Some of the winged females fly to other plants and start new colonies. Toward the end of the summer, both male and female aphids are born. The males and females of this generation mate, and the female lays eggs that will hatch in spring.

◀ **A winged female aphid giving birth to live young.**

Most aphid young grow inside the female aphid and are born alive. The soft newborn looks like a very small adult aphid.

▶ **The female aphid and her young.**

The wingless newborns live and feed on the same plant where they are born. Some winged aphids travel to a different kind of plant to live, but they return to their first home when they are ready to produce their young.

◀ **A young nymph.**

The first aphids of the season are all wingless females. They are also the only aphids that emerge from eggs.

▶ **A wingless female giving birth.**

The female aphids that give birth to live young do not mate with male aphids. Having young without mating is called parthenogenesis.

All aphids go through physical changes before they become fully grown adult aphids. The physical changing is called a metamorphosis. All insects go through some kind of metamorphosis. Sometimes a young insect looks different from the adult and goes through four separate changes before it is an adult. This is called a complete metamorphosis. Young aphids, or nymphs, look like the adult but are smaller. Aphids go through an incomplete, or simple, metamorphosis. The main physical change is an increase in size.

As the aphid nymph grows, its skin becomes too small for its body. The nymph must shed, or molt, its old skin. Soon the tightly stretched skin splits down the back, and the nymph wriggles out. The soft new skin hardens and forms a protective covering for the nymph. But the new skin will also become too small. The nymph will molt several more times before it is fully grown.

◀ Dairying ants visit an aphid colony.

The ants journey from their nearby nest to collect honeydew from the aphids. Although these ants eat other insects, honeydew is their main food.

▶ An ant milking an aphid.

The ant uses its antennae to stroke, or milk, the abdomen of the aphid. The milking by the ants increases the amount of honeydew the aphid excretes.

It is unusual for one kind of insect to share its home with another kind of insect. But aphids that produce honeydew welcome ants into their colony. The aphids supply the ants with sweet honeydew, and the ants protect the aphids from predators, other insects that want to feed on the aphids.

Ants, called dairying ants, visit the aphid colony near their nest to collect honeydew. The ants "milk" the honeydew from the aphids by stroking the abdomen of the aphids with their feelers, or antennae. When the honeydew is excreted, the ants eagerly lick it up.

Some aphids have developed a very special relationship with ants and depend on the ants to survive. The eggs of the corn root aphid are gathered by certain field ants and carried to the ants' nest, where they spend the winter. In the spring, the ants carry the young aphids to the roots of weeds so they can feed. Later, the ants move the adult aphids to the roots of young corn plants.

◄ **A brightly colored syrphid fly.**

The striped syrphid fly resembles a bee or a wasp. It is hovering over a field of flowers.

▼ **The female syrphid laying an egg.**

The syrphid fly lands quickly on a flower bud and lays her egg among the aphids.

Not all visitors to the aphid colony are as helpful as the ant. An insect called the syrphid fly is a dangerous enemy of the aphid. Because this fly can be found wherever there are flowers, it is often called the flower fly. Many syrphid flies look like bees or wasps. They not only feed on flowers, but they also lap up the aphid honeydew from the surface of the leaves.

On a summer day, the syrphid fly can be seen hovering in the air, feeding on the flowers near an aphid colony. Every once in a while it will dart down to the aphid colony. When it darts down, it lays one of its eggs among the aphids. The egg is held to the leaf by the sticky honeydew on the surface. When the egg hatches, the syrphid larva crawls out and begins to feed on the aphids.

▼ A syrphid fly egg in an aphid colony.

The female syrphid fly lays her egg in an aphid colony. After the larva emerges, it will feed on the aphids. The arrow in the photograph points to the long white syrphid fly egg that is as big as the young aphids.

▲ A newly emerged syrphid larva (arrow) and egg case.

▶ The syrphid fly larva feeding on an aphid.

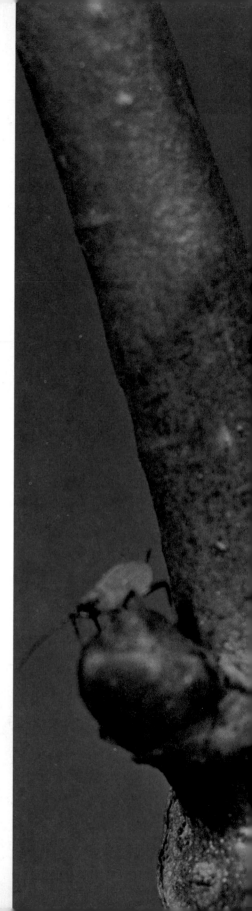

The syrphid fly larva is a ferocious predator. It seizes an aphid with its sharp mouthparts and raises the front of its body, lifting the aphid into the air. Then with strong gulping movements, the larva sucks out the body fluids of the aphid. The hungry syrphid fly larva moves through the colony, feeding on one aphid after another. One larva can eat almost a thousand aphids in just a few weeks.

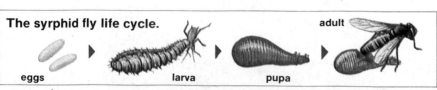

The syrphid fly life cycle.

adult

eggs   larva   pupa

▲ **Feeding on aphids.**

When the hungry ladybird beetle larvae emerge, they immediately start to feed on the helpless aphids. The larvae spend several weeks feeding on aphids (left) before they start the pupal stage. Adult ladybird beetles also feed on aphids (right).

Ladybird beetles, sometimes called ladybugs, also lay their eggs in a colony of aphids. The female ladybird beetle lays groups of yellowish eggs on the underside of the leaf. In about seven days, the larvae emerge from the eggs. The larvae search the plant for aphids. And even though new ladybird beetle larvae are smaller than the aphids, they have no trouble capturing and eating the aphids.

In about two weeks the growing ladybird beetle larvae stop eating and begin the pupal stage. During the pupal stage they are attached to a leaf near the aphid colony. In about a week, ladybird beetles emerge as adults. The adults also feed on the aphids.

◀ **A ladybird beetle laying its eggs.**

The ladybird beetle lays many eggs at a time. She places the eggs close to an aphid colony.

The ladybird beetle life cycle.

eggs   larva   pupa   adult

◄ A spider eating a ladybird beetle.

Many spiders eat the enemies of aphids. The spider hunts the ladybird beetle. The spider injects the beetle with a substance that keeps the beetle from moving and then quickly sucks its body fluids.

► A spider eating a syrphid fly.

The syrphid fly is caught by a spider that looks like an ant. The syrphid fly does not fly away from the spider because it looks like a friendly ant.

A huge number of aphids are born every summer. If all the young lived, they could cause a lot of damage. Whole fields of crops can be destroyed by a large aphid population.

But a huge population of aphids usually does not build up because the aphid has so many enemies. And the insects that feed on aphids also are hunted by other insects. Spiders feed on aphids, but they also feed on the syrphid flies and the ladybird beetles that hunt aphids. A food chain is formed when the aphid is eaten by the ladybird beetle and then the ladybird beetle is eaten by the spider. Because of the food chain, there aren't too many of one kind of insect.

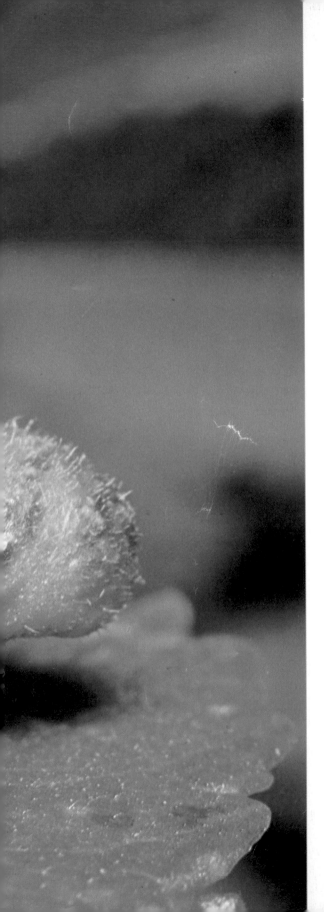

Some species of aphids secrete a chemical into plants as they feed. The chemical causes the plant to grow in an unusual way. A balloon-like growth develops on the plant. The growth is called a gall. Inside the gall, the aphid colony forms. The aphids grow as they feed on the walls of the gall. There is an opening to the outside, and when the gall becomes crowded, the winged aphids leave to form other gall colonies.

◄ **Plant galls made by aphids.**

▼ **Inside a plant gall.**

When a plant gall is opened, an aphid colony can be seen inside. The aphids are covered by a white, waxy substance that they secrete.

▼ **A lacewing stalking an aphid.** A lacewing hides under leaves and small pieces of dried-up plants. When the aphid is close, the lacewing uses its strong mandibles to grab and eat the aphid.

▲ **Lacewing eggs.**

The eggs swing gently from the long thin threads attached to the plant.

▲ **A lacewing larva feeding on an aphid.**

The lacewing larva stabs the aphid with sharp hollow pincers and sucks the fluid from the aphid.

Like the ladybird beetle, both the adults and larvae of the lacewing feed on aphids. The female lacewing lays her eggs near an aphid colony. She attaches them to the plant with long thin threads. When the young larvae hatch, they immediately seek out the aphids. Some of the larvae pile small dead pieces of plants and leaves on their backs to hide themselves as they hunt the aphids. The mouthparts of the larva look like two long curved claws. These sharp jaws, or mandibles, are hollow. When the larva catches an aphid it pierces it with the hollow pincers and sucks the fluid from the aphid. The larva's attack on the aphid is so fierce that it is often called an aphid lion.

The lacewing life cycle.

eggs   larva   pupa   adult

◄ Wasps laying eggs inside other insects.

Some wasps grow to adults inside other insects. These wasps are called parasites. Different kinds of parasitic wasps lay their eggs in different insects. The wasp in the upper photo lays eggs in syrphid fly larvae. The wasp in the lower left photo lays eggs in ladybird beetles. The wasp in the lower right photo lays eggs in the bodies of aphids.

► Wasp pupae inside a syrphid fly larva.

The dead syrphid larva has been the home for growing parasitic wasps.

It is not unusual for a predator like the wasp to lay its eggs near an aphid colony. But some wasps do more. They lay their eggs inside aphids. They also lay their eggs inside aphid predators in the colony.

The wasp sticks a long tube that extends from its abdomen, called an ovipositor, into the aphid. An egg travels through the ovipositor into the aphid. When the larva comes out of the egg, it feeds inside the body of the aphid. The aphid becomes a hard swollen ball. Before long, its color darkens, and it dies. The wasp goes through a complete metamorphosis inside the aphid. The adult wasp emerges through a hole it cuts in the top of the aphid's abdomen.

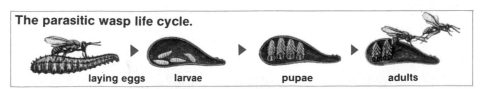

The parasitic wasp life cycle.

laying eggs   larvae   pupae   adults

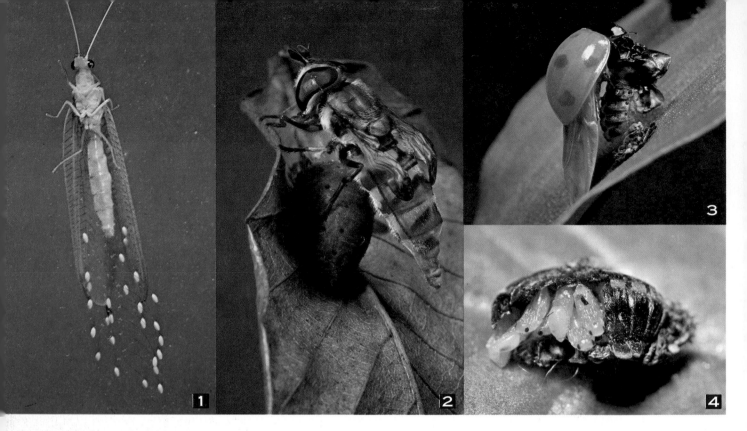

▲ **Insects that prey on aphids.** Aphid predators make their homes close to aphid colonies. The most common predators are (**1**) lacewings, (**2**) syrphid flies, (**3**) ladybird beetles, and (**4**) parasitic wasps.

Many enemies surround the aphid colony. The aphids without wings can do little to escape from their predators. Even the aphids with wings cannot always get away. If the winged aphid is molting, the wings may still be soft and crumpled against its body. While it waits in the sun for its wings to unfold and harden, it is defenseless and is easy prey for enemies.

Most aphids have one defense against enemies. When an aphid is attacked, it secretes a substance from two tubes on its abdomen. The substance is called an alarm pheromone. When it gets into the attacker's mouth, it irritates the attacker so much that it often releases the aphid. The pheromone also acts as a warning to nearby aphids. When they sense the pheromone with their antennae, they move away from the attacker.

▼ A winged aphid nymph molting. The nymph has emerged from the pale brown skin left on the leaf. When the nymph's transparent wings stretch out and harden, there will be a set of large front wings and a set of small back wings. The winged aphid is able to escape its predators as well as fly to other plants to start new colonies.

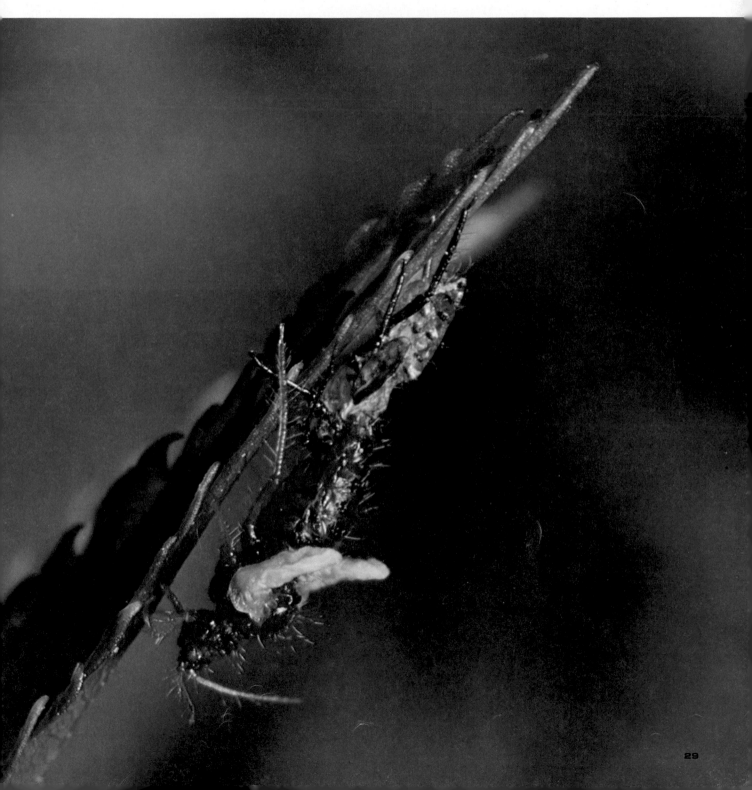

As autumn approaches and the weather gets cooler, plants make less and less sap. The plants stop growing and begin to turn brown. Before long the aphids will be left without food. With a rush of activity, the male and female aphids mate. After mating, the female aphid lays her eggs on a plant. That plant will be food for the young aphids when they are born in the spring. The colony quickly becomes filled with hundreds of eggs.

The adult aphids cannot survive the cold weather and lack of food. When the aphids die, insects that prey on aphids are also left without food. So they hibernate, or rest, through the winter. They emerge in spring to feed on the new aphids.

The future aphids are safe in their eggs through the winter. In spring, the eggs will hatch and wingless female aphids will emerge to start another generation of aphids.

◄ **Aphids and their eggs.**

Hundreds of eggs are laid in autumn after the male and female aphids have mated. Autumn is the only time of the year that eggs are laid by the female.

▶ **A ladybird beetle ready to hibernate.**

When the last aphids of summer die, ladybird beetles and other aphid predators are left without food. The predators hibernate through the winter and emerge in spring with the newly hatched aphids.

GLOSSARY

honeydew—the sweet liquid waste product excreted by some insects. (pp. 6, 13)

mandibles—the jaws of an insect that are used for biting and chewing. (pp. 24, 25)

metamorphosis—a process of development during which physical changes take place. Complete metamorphosis involves four stages: egg, larva, pupa, and adult. Incomplete metamorphosis occurs in three stages: egg, nymph, and adult. (pp. 10, 27)

molt—to shed the outer skin. (pp. 10, 28, 29)

ovipositor—an egg-laying tube that extends from the tip of an insect's abdomen. (p. 27)

parasite—an animal that gets its food by living on or in another animal. (p. 27)

parthenogenesis—the ability of a female animal to produce young without mating with a male. (p. 10)

predator—an animal that hunts or kills other animals for food. (pp. 13, 16, 27)

sap—the fluid in a plant that brings nourishment to all parts of the plant. (pp. 4, 6)

species—a group of animals that scientists have identified as having common characteristics. (pp. 6, 23)